P9-CEZ-256

*True Love*

# TRUE LOVE

## A Practice
## for Awakening
## the Heart

THICH NHAT HANH

*Translated by*
Sherab Chödzin Kohn

SHAMBHALA
*Boston & London*
2004

SHAMBHALA PUBLICATIONS, INC.
Horticultural Hall
Shambhala Publications
300 Massachusetts Avenue
Boston, Massachusetts 02115
*www.shambhala.com*

© 1997 by Éditions Terre du Ciel

Originally published in French under the
title *Vivre en Pleine Conscience*

Published by arrangement with the United
Buddhist Church, Inc., POB 182, Hartland
Four Corners, VT 05049 USA.
Translation © 2004 by Shambhala Publications

All rights reserved. No part of this book may
be reproduced in any form or by any means, electronic
or mechanical, including photocopying, recording,
or by any information storage and retrieval system,
without permission in writing from the publisher.

9 8 7 6 5 4 3 2

Printed in the United States of America

♾ This edition is printed on acid-free paper that
meets the American National Standards
Institute z39.48 Standard.

Distributed in the United States by Random
House, Inc., and in Canada by Random
House of Canada Ltd

See page 109 for Library of Congress
Cataloging-in-Publication Data.

# Contents

# Contents

# Contents

# Contents

*True Love*

# The Four
# Aspects of Love

According to Buddhism, there are four elements of true love.

The first is *maitri*, which can be translated as loving-kindness or benevolence. Loving-kindness is not only the desire to make someone happy, to bring joy to a beloved person; it is the *ability* to bring joy and happiness to the person you love, because even if your intention is to love this person, your love might make him or her suffer.

Training is needed in order to love properly; and to be able to give happiness and joy, you must practice *deep looking* directed toward the person you love. Because if you do not understand this person, you cannot love properly. Understanding is the essence of love. If you cannot understand, you cannot love. That is the message of the Buddha. If a husband, for example, does not understand his wife's deepest troubles, her deepest aspirations, if he does not understand her suffering, he will not be able to love her in the right way. Without understanding, love is an impossible thing.

What must we do in order to understand a person? We must have time; we must practice looking deeply into this person. We must be there, attentive; we must observe, we must look deeply. And the fruit of this looking deeply is called understanding. Love is a true thing if it is made up of a substance called understanding.

The second element of true love is compassion, *karuna*. This is not only the desire to ease the pain of another person, but the *ability* to do so. You must practice deep looking in order to gain a good understanding of the nature of the suffering of this person, in order to be able to help him or her to change. Knowledge and understanding are always at the root of the practice. The practice of understanding is the practice of meditation. To meditate is to look deeply into the heart of things.

The third element of true love is joy, *mudita*. If there is no joy in love, it is not true love. If you are suffering all the time, if you cry all the time, and if you make the person you love cry, this is not really love—it is even the opposite. If there is no joy in your love, you can be sure that it is not true love.

The fourth element is *upeksha*, equanimity or freedom. In true love, you attain freedom. When you love, you bring freedom to the person you love. If the opposite is true, it is not true love. You must love in such a way that the person you love feels free, not only outside but also inside. "Dear one, do you have enough space in your heart and all around you?" This is an intelligent question for testing out whether your love is something real.

*Love Is
Being There*

To LOVE, IN THE CONTEXT OF BUDDHISM, is above all to be there. But being there is not an easy thing. Some training is necessary, some practice. If you are not there, how can you love? Being there is very much an art, the art of meditation, because meditating is bringing your true presence to the here and now. The question that arises is: Do you have time to love?

I know a boy of twelve whose father asked him one day: "Son, what would you like for your birthday present?" The boy did not know how to answer his father, who was a very rich man, able to buy anything for his son. But the boy did not want anything except his father's presence. Because the role the father played kept him very busy, he did not have time to devote to his wife and children. Being rich is an obstacle to loving. When you are rich, you want to continue to be rich, and so you end up devoting all your time, all your energy in your daily life, to staying rich. If this father were to understand what true love is, he would do whatever is necessary to find time for his son and his wife.

The most precious gift you can give to

the one you love is your true presence. What must we do to really be there? Those who have practiced Buddhist meditation know that meditating is above all being present: to yourself, to those you love, to life.

So I would propose a very simple practice to you, the practice of mindful breathing: "Breathing—I know that I am breathing in; breathing—I know that I am breathing out." If you do that with a little concentration, then you will be able to really be there, because in our daily life our mind and our body are rarely together. Our body might be there, but our mind is somewhere else. Maybe you are lost in regrets about the past, maybe in worries about the future, or else you are preoccupied with your plans, with anger or with jealousy. And so your mind is not really there with your body.

Between the mind and the body, there is something that can serve as a bridge. The moment you begin to practice mindful breathing, your body and your mind begin to come together with one another. It takes only ten to twenty seconds to accomplish this miracle called oneness of body and mind. With mindful breathing, you can bring body and mind together in the present moment, and every one of us can do it, even a child.

The Buddha left us an absolutely essential text, the *Anapanasati Sutta*, or *Discourse on the Practice of Mindful Breathing*. If you really want to practice Buddhist meditation, you must study this text.

If the father I was talking about had known that, he would have begun to breathe in and breathe out mindfully, and then one or two minutes later, he would have approached his son, he would have looked at him with a smile, and he would have said this: "My dear, I am here for you." This is the greatest gift you can give to someone you love.

In Buddhism we talk about mantras. A mantra is a magic formula that, once it is uttered, can entirely change a situation, our mind, our body, or a person. But this magic formula must be spoken in a state of concentration, that is to say, a state in which body and mind are absolutely in a state of unity. What you say then, in this state of being, becomes a mantra.

So I am going to present to you a very effective mantra, not in Sanskrit or Tibetan, but in English: "Dear one, I am here for you." Perhaps this evening you will try for a few minutes to practice mindful breathing in order to bring your body and mind together. You will approach the person you love and with this mindfulness, with this concentration, you will look into his or her eyes, and you will begin to utter this formula: "Dear one, I am really here for you." You must say that with your body and with your mind at the same time, and then you will see the transformation.

Do you have enough time to love? Can you make sure that in your everyday life you have a little time to love? We do not have much time together; we are too busy. In the morning while eating breakfast, we do not look at the person we love, we do not have enough time for it. We eat very quickly while thinking about other things, and sometimes we even hold a newspaper that hides the face of the person we love. In the evening when we come home, we are too tired to be able to look at the person we love.

We must bring about a revolution in our way of living our everyday lives, because our happiness, our lives, are within ourselves.

you love someone and you continue to ignore his or her presence, this is not true love. Perhaps your intention is not to ignore this person, but the way you act, look, and speak does not manifest the desire to recognize the presence of the other. When we are loved, we wish the other to recognize our presence, and this is a very important practice. You must do whatever is necessary to be able to do this: recognize the presence of the person you love several times each day.

To attain this goal, it is also necessary to practice oneness of body and mind. Practice an inbreath and an outbreath three times, five times, seven times; then you approach this person, you look at him or her mindfully, with a smile, and you begin to say the second mantra: "Dear one, I know that you are here, and it makes me very happy." If you practice in this way, with a lot of concentration and mindfulness, you will see that this person will open immediately, like a flower blossoming. To be loved is to be recognized, and you can do that several times a day. It is not difficult at all, and it is a true meditation.

Whatever you do mindfully is meditation. When you touch a flower, you can touch it with your fingers, but better yet, you can touch it mindfully, with your full awareness. "Breathing in—I know that the flower is there; breathing out—I smile at the flower." While you are practicing in this way, you are really there and at the same time, the flower is really there. If you are not really there, nothing is there. The sunset is something marvelous and so is the full moon, but since you are not really there, the sunset is not for you. From time to time, I let myself look at the full moon; I take a deep breath in and a deep breath out, and I practice: "I know you are there, and I am very glad about it." I practice that with the full moon, with the cherry blossoms . . . We are surrounded by miracles, but we have to recognize them; otherwise there is no life.

The Buddha told us this: "The past is no longer there, the future is not here yet; there is only one moment in which life is available and that is the present moment." To meditate is to bring body and mind back to the present moment so that you do not miss your appointment with life.

Albert Camus wrote a novel, *The Stranger*, in which his character, Meursault, is condemned to death. Three days before his execution, he is able for the first time in his life to touch the blue sky. He is in his cell, he is looking at the ceiling. He discovers a square of blue sky appearing through the skylight. Strangely enough, a man forty years of age is able to see the blue sky for the first time. Of course, he had looked at the stars and the blue sky more than once before, but this time it was for real. We might not know how to touch the blue sky in such a profound way. The moment of awareness Camus describes is mindfulness: Suddenly you are able to touch life.

In Buddhism, the energy that helps us to touch life deeply is called *smrti*, the energy of mindfulness. Everyone possesses a seed (*bija*) of this energy. If we practice mindful breathing, we can generate this energy.

When you breathe in, you recognize at that moment that this is an inbreath; when you breathe out, you are aware of the fact that this is an outbreath. Recognizing what is there in the present moment is attention.

her, with your body and mind unified, with concentration, and you utter the third mantra: "Dear one, I know that you are suffering, that is why I am here for you." Because when we are suffering, we have a strong need for the presence of the person we love. If we are suffering and the man or woman we love ignores us, then we suffer more. So what we can do—right away—is to manifest our true presence to the beloved person and say the mantra with all our mindfulness: "Dear one, I know that you are suffering, that is why I am here for you." Even before you actually do something to help, the person you love is relieved. Your presence is a miracle, your understanding of his or her pain is a miracle, and you are able to offer this aspect of your love immediately.

Really try to be there, for yourself, for life, for the people that you love. Recognize the presence of those who live in the same place as you and try to be there when one of them is suffering, because your presence is so precious for this person. In this way you will be practicing love twenty-four hours a day.

you would be suffering less. But in this case, it is the person I love most in the world who said that to me, who did that to me, and I am suffering more. I am deeply hurt by the fact that my suffering was caused by the person I love the most. I feel like going to my room, closing the door, staying by myself, and crying. I refuse to go to him or her to ask for help. So now it is pride that is the obstacle.

According to the teaching of the Buddha, in true love there is no place for pride. If you are suffering, every time you are suffering you must go to the person in question and ask for his or her help. That is true love. Do not let pride keep you apart. If you think your love for this person is true love, you must overcome your pride; you must always go to him or her. That is why I have invented this mantra for you. Practice so as to bring about oneness of your body and mind before going to the person to say the fourth mantra: "Dear one, I am suffering, please help." This is very simple, but very hard to do.

I would like to tell you a story from my country. A young man went off to war, leaving his pregnant wife behind. Two years later, he was able to return home, and the young woman went with their young son to meet her husband. They cried together out of joy. In Vietnam, in our tradition, when an event of this kind takes place, it has to be announced to the ancestors. So the young father asked his wife to go to the market to buy the things that are needed for the offering that is placed on the altar to the ancestors. Such an altar is found in every house. Each morning we burn a stick of incense to our ancestors on this altar, and in this way we make a connection with them. Burning this incense, adorning the altar with photographs of our ancestors, and dusting the shrine off are very important gestures. These are moments in which we come in contact with our ancestors. There are people living in the world who are completely uprooted because they do not practice such a turning toward their ancestors.

So the young wife went off to the market. During this time, the young father was trying to convince his child to call him Daddy. The little boy refused: "Mister, you're not my daddy. My daddy is somebody else. He visits us every night and my mommy talks to him every night, and very often she cries with him. And every time my mommy sits down, he sits down too. Every time she lies down, he lies down too." After he heard these words, the young father's happiness entirely evaporated. His heart turned into a block of ice. He felt hurt, deeply humiliated, and that is why, when his wife came home, he would no longer look at her or speak a word to her. He ignored her. The woman herself began to suffer; she felt humiliated, hurt. When the offering was placed on the altar, the young father burned the incense, recited the prayers to the ancestors, and did the four traditional prostrations. Then he picked the mat up instead of leaving it there for his wife so she could do the four prostrations in her turn. In his mind he thought that she was not qualified to present herself before the ancestors, and she was humiliated by this.

After the ceremony, he didn't stay at the house to eat but went to the village and spent the day in a bar. He tried to forget his her shadow: "My dear one, you are so far away from me. How can I raise my child all by myself? . . . You must come back home soon." She would cry, and of course every time she sat down, the shadow would also sit down. Now the husband's false perception was no longer there, but it was too late—his wife was already dead.

A misperception is something that can destroy an entire family. The Buddha told us a number of times that we are subject to misperceptions in our everyday life. Therefore we have to pay close attention to our perceptions. There are people who hang on to their misperceptions for ten or twenty years, and during this time they continue to suffer and make other people suffer.

Why did the young father not want to talk this thing over with his wife? Because pride got in between them. If he had asked his wife: "Who is this person who came every night? Our child told me about him. I am suffering so much, my darling, you have to help me. Explain to me who this person is." If he had done that, his wife would have had a chance to explain, and the drama could have been avoided. However, it was not only his fault, but that of his young wife as well. She could have come to him and asked him the reason for his change in attitude: "Husband, why don't you look at me anymore, why don't you talk to me? Have I done something awful that I deserve such treatment? I am suffering so much, dear husband, you have to help me."

She did not do this, and I do not want you to make the same mistake in your everyday life. We are subject to misperceptions every day, so we have to pay attention. Every time you think it is somebody else who is causing the suffering, you must re-member this story. You must always check things out by going to the person in ques-tion and asking for his or her help: "Dear one, I am suffering so much, help me please."

# Deep Listening

YOU HAVE RECEIVED THE TRANSMISSION of the four mantras for the practice of true love. You know that it is not difficult to practice these mantras. You should learn them by heart, and you must have the courage, the wisdom, and the joy to practice them.

But if the situation has already become

extremely difficult, what can you do? What can you do if love has already caused too much suffering between the two of you? For appearances, you behave so that others will think that you two are still living together and that you still find joy in living together, but in reality there is no more joy, there is no more happiness, there isn't even communication anymore. You have lost the capacity to listen and to speak. Communication has become difficult, in fact impossible. What can you do in a situation like this? The two of you have been living together and making each other suffer.

According to Buddhism, we are dealing with *samyojana*, the lump of suffering within us that is translated as an "internal formation." When you say something that makes another person suffer, that person develops an "internal formation." If that person is trained in Buddhism, he or she will know how to untie that knot. If not, he will let it remain there in the depths of his consciousness. If you are a person who practices mindfulness, you will be aware that a knot has been formed in the person you love and you will know how to untie it.

Every day we say or do things that might leave behind "internal formations" in the person we love. Following that, then the suffering and pain can grow, and the person we love turns into something like a bomb that might explode at any moment. A few words are all it takes to trigger anger in this person, who you are afraid to approach and who you are afraid to talk to because he or she has become a bomb loaded with too much suffering. When you try to get away from him or her, this person thinks that you do so out of contempt and we can cultivate awareness, and we can cultivate compassion—and that way we will be able to sit there and listen to the other. The other suffers as long as he is in need of someone to listen to him; and you—you are the person who can do it. If someone has to have recourse to a psychotherapist, it is because no one in his house can listen. A psychotherapist should be able to sit there and really listen, but I know therapists who have suffered too much and do not truly have the ability to listen to their clients.

So if we love someone, we should train in being able to listen. By listening with calm and understanding, we can ease the suffering of another person. An hour spent in this way can already relieve a great deal of another person's pain. In Plum Village, our practice place, deep listening is a very important practice. Every week we get to-

There are pacifists who can write protest letters of great condemnation but who are incapable of writing a love letter. You have to write in such a way that the other person is receptive toward reading; you have to speak in such a way that the other person is receptive toward listening. If you do not, it is not worth the trouble to write or to speak. To write in such a way is to practice meditation.

I remember a young American who came to us to practice. One day he was asked to write a letter to his mother, which was easy for him. On the other hand, it was impossible for him to write a letter to his father. His father had died, but he still suffered every time he thought of him. Just the idea of picking up a pen to write to his father already caused him a great deal of suffering.

I proposed the following practice to him. For one week he practiced mindful breathing, saying to himself, "Breathing in—I see myself as a child of five." When one is a little boy of five, one is very fragile and vulnerable. As he was breathing in, he saw himself as the object of his own compassion. During the second week, he meditated on his father: "Breathing in—I see my dad as a little child of five; breathing out—I smile at the little boy who was my dad."

For a whole week, the young American practiced very faithfully and very enthusiastically. He put a photo of his father on the table and every time he walked into the room and looked at it, he practiced mindful breathing. He had never imagined that his father could have been a child of five. Suddenly the young man acknowledged the presence of his father as a little boy. It was the first time that he realized that his father had suffered as a little boy, and suddenly he felt compassion. Finally one evening he found it possible to write a first letter to his father. That transformed him completely, and now he has peace in his heart.

Meditation is the practice of looking deeply into the nature of your suffering and your joy. Through the energy of mindfulness, through concentration, looking deeply into the nature of our suffering makes it possible for us to see the deep causes of that suffering. If you can keep mindfulness and concentration alive, then looking deeply will reveal to you the true nature of your pain. And freedom will arise as a result of your sustaining a deep vision into the nature of your pain. Solidity, freedom, calm, and joy are the fruits of meditation.

yourself, and you will be able to transform negative energies into joy and peace. The Buddha said this: "The object of your practice should first of all be yourself. Your love for the other, your ability to love another person, depends on your ability to love yourself." If you are not able to take care of yourself, if you are not able to accept yourself, how could you accept another person and how could you love him or her? So it is necessary to come back to yourself in order to be able to achieve the transformation.

Each of us is a king who reigns over a very vast territory that has five rivers. The first river is our body, which we do not know well enough. The second is the river of sensations. Each sensation is a drop of water in this river. There are pleasant sensations, others that are unpleasant, and neutral sensations. To meditate is to sit down on the bank of the river of sensations and identify each sensation as it arises. The third is the river of perceptions, which it is necessary to observe. You must look deeply into their nature in order to understand. The fourth is the river of mental formations, of which there are fifty-one.[*] And finally, the fifth is the river of consciousness.

Our territory is really very vast, but we are not responsible kings or queens. We always try to dodge away and we do not keep up a real surveillance of our territory. We have the feeling that there are

---

[*] In this passage Thich Nhat Hanh presents the five *skandhas* or aggregates. According to Buddhist philosophy, these are the elements that constitute "personality" or selfhood: form, sensation, perception, mental formations, and consciousness. Mental formations include mental activities such as discrimination, happiness, equanimity, resolve, compulsion, concentration, and so forth.—Ed.

immense conflicts there, too much suffering, too much pain—that is the reason we are very hesitant to get back to our territory. Our daily practice consists in running away. If we have a moment free, we will make use of it to watch television or read a magazine article so we will not have to go back to our territory. We are afraid of the suffering that is inside us, afraid of war and conflicts.

The practice of mindfulness, the practice of meditation, consists of coming back to ourselves in order to restore peace and harmony. The energy with which we can do this is the energy of mindfulness. Mindfulness is a kind of energy that carries with it concentration, understanding, and love. If we come back to ourselves to restore peace and harmony, then helping another person will be a much easier thing.

Caring for yourself, reestablishing peace in yourself, is the basic condition for helping someone else. So that the other can stop being a bomb, a source of pain for ourselves and others, you really have to help him to defuse the bomb. To be able to provide help, we have to have a little calm, a little joy, a little compassion in ourselves. This is what we get from mindfulness in everyday life, because mindfulness is not something that is only done in a meditation hall; it is also done in the kitchen, in the garden, when we are on the telephone, when we are driving a car, when we are doing the dishes.

If you can do it this way, three weeks are enough to transform the pain inside you, to bring back your joy in living, to cultivate the energy of compassion with which you can help the person you love. The practice of being there with what is

# The Energy of
# Mindfulness

Understanding is the fruit of meditation. When we practice deep looking directed toward the heart of reality, we receive help, we receive understanding, we receive the wisdom that makes us free. If there is a deep pain within you, meditate.

Meditating is not trying to run away,

trying to ignore the presence of the pain, but on the contrary, it is looking at it face-to-face. You have to practice deep looking directed toward the nature of this pain, because for Buddhists, we are joy, but we are also pain; we are understanding, but we are also ignorance. Meditating is not transforming oneself into a battlefield where one side is fighting another, where good fights against evil. This is not Buddhist meditation. Buddhist meditation is based on the principle of nonduality. This means that if we are mindfulness, if we are love, we are also ignorance, we are also suffering, and there is no reason to suppress anything at all.

When the seed of anger manifests on the level of our conscious mind, our immediate awareness, it is because the seed of anger is in the depths of our consciousness, and then we begin to suffer. Our immediate awareness is something like our living room. The task of the meditator is not to chase away or to suppress the energy of anger that is there but rather to invite another energy that will be able to care for the anger.

You can use the method of mindful breathing to make the seed of this other energy grow inside you. It will then manifest in the form of energy, and this energy will embrace your energy of anger like a mother taking a baby in her arms. Then there is only tenderness, there is no fighting with, or discriminating against, the pain. The purpose of the practice of mindful breathing is to help to give birth to this precious energy called mindfulness and to keep it alive.

We have already spoken of this energy that illuminates us. Mindfulness is like a light, enabling concentration to really be there, and that also makes it possible for us to look deeply into the heart of things. From this looking deeply is born deep vision, understanding. Mindfulness brings concentration, understanding, love, and freedom.

If you are a Christian, you could say that this energy we are talking about is known as the Holy Spirit, the energy that is sent to us by God. Wherever this energy exists, there is attention, understanding, love, compassion. And this energy has the power to heal. Since Jesus embodies this energy, he has the ability to heal whoever he touches. When Jesus touches people, he touches them with the energy of the Holy Spirit. It is not touching his clothing that has the power to heal. We could say that when the energy of compassion and love touches us, healing establishes itself.

In Buddhism we say that mindfulness is the energy of Buddha. The seed of mindfulness is the baby Buddha that is in us. This precious seed can be buried very deeply under several layers of suffering and ignorance. We begin by looking for, by touching, this seed of mindfulness, and everybody knows that all of us have this precious seed in us.

When you drink water, if you are aware of the fact that you are drinking water, mindfulness is there. Mindfulness is the energy that makes it possible for us to be aware of what is happening in the present moment.

When you breathe in and you are aware that you are breathing in, mindfulness is room," like a mother tenderly embracing your pain. With that energy of mindfulness, you are doing the true practice of meditation with regard to your pain, your emotions. If you are able to maintain mindfulness for five or ten minutes, you will experience some relief right away.

When the mother hears her baby crying, she puts down whatever she has in her hands, she goes into its room, and takes the baby in her arms. The moment the baby is lifted into the mother's arms, the energy of wisdom already begins to penetrate into the baby's body. The mother does not know yet what is the matter with the baby, but the fact that she has it in her arms already gives her child some relief. The baby stops crying. Then the mother continues to hold the baby in her arms, she continues to offer it the energy of tenderness, and able to keep this up, the result could be there, maybe, in three or four minutes. The next time you are angry, practice doing walking meditation in a natural setting, for example. You breathe and you concentrate solely on breathing: "Breathing in—I know that I am breathing in; breathing out—I know that I am breathing out." After a minute or two, you practice this way: "Breathing in—I know that I am angry; breathing out—I know that the anger is still in me." Ten minutes later, you will feel better. It is a sure thing, on condition that the energy of mindfulness is really there; and if you keep it up, concentration—and not only concentration but also deep looking—will also be there. You will be able to look deeply at the true nature of your anger. This discovery, this understanding, this wisdom, will liberate you from your pain.

A lot of the time we turn on the television, we read novels, we make phone calls—just to keep pain from making its appearance in our "living room." We practice the politics of subversion, we carry out a kind of boycott toward the negative seeds within us, and after a certain amount of time of doing this we create a situation of bad circulation. You know that when the blood is not circulating well in our body, we experience pains—headaches, for example. So then we try getting massages or taking medicines, because good circulation is essential for our health. The same thing is true with regard to our consciousness. If we practice the politics of repression and suppression, then we create a situation of bad circulation for our mental formations, such as fear, anger, despair, suffering. And because things are not circulating properly in our conscious mind, then the symptoms of mental illness appear: depression and stress.

We should not adopt this boycott policy. On the contrary we should open our door so that our suffering can come out. We are afraid of doing that, but Buddhism teaches us that we should not be afraid, because we have available to us an energy that should help us to care for our pain—the energy of mindfulness.

If we practice cultivating this energy of mindfulness every day, we will have enough of it to take care of our pains. Every time pain manifests, we will welcome it. We will really be there to take care of it, and the energy needed to take care of it is without a doubt the energy of mindfulness: "I am here for you, dear one, I am here for you." That is one of the four mantras we learned. This means that the mother is there for the baby, the energy of mindfulness is there to embrace the energy of pain.

So we have to train every day in cultivating this energy of mindfulness. But we need friends, brothers and sisters in the Dharma, to be able to do this easily. That is why in Buddhism we talk about the practice of taking refuge in the sangha: "I take refuge in the sangha." The sangha is a practice community in which brothers and sisters in the Dharma practice the cultivation of mindfulness daily: when they eat, when they drink, when they wash the dishes, when they work in the garden, when they drive a car—and not just during times of sitting meditation. So it is necessary to have a bit of training and a sangha, that is, a community of practice.

In the tradition it is said that a practitioner who leaves the sangha is like a tiger who has left the mountains and gone down to the plains. If the animal does that, he will be killed by humans; and if the practitioner of meditation does not take refuge in a community, in a sangha, he will abandon his practice after a few months. Thus a sangha is absolutely necessary for continuing one's practice.

# The Principle of
# Nonduality

W HEN OUR PAIN COMES UP, IT REMAINS
for a period of time at the level of the conscious mind, in our "living room." After a
short stay there, it goes back to its usual
habitat, the *alaya* consciousness,* where it

---

* In Buddhist thought, consciousness is sometimes described
as having eight levels. *Alaya* is the fundamental (continued)

takes the form of a seed; and now it will be a little bit weaker. It will always be a little bit weaker after having been embraced by the energy of mindfulness. The next time it manifests, we will receive it the same way; we will care for it the same way with the energy of mindfulness, and then it will return to the depths, weaker still. It loses energy every time it is embraced by the energy of mindfulness, which is really a mother.

The door is already open; mental formations can now flow freely. And if you practice that for a few weeks, the symptoms of mental illness will disappear. This is because you are now in a situation where you have good circulation in your psyche. That is why the Buddha taught us to invite fear

consciousness that supports and nourishes the seven others. It is sometimes called the "storehouse consciousness," since it contains every kind of seed and its primary function is to preserve all the seeds. —Ed.

into our mindful consciousness and care for it every day.

There is no battle between good and evil, positive and negative; there is only the care given by the big brother to the little brother. In Buddhist meditation, we observe, we act in a nondualistic fashion, and thus the waste materials of the conscious mind can always be transformed into flowers of compassion, love, and peace. Our consciousness is a living thing, something organic in nature. There are always waste materials and flowers in us. The gardener who is familiar with organic gardening is constantly on the alert to save the waste materials because he knows how to transform them into compost and then transform that compost into flowers and vegetables. So be grateful for your pains, be grateful for suffering—you will need them.

We have to learn the art of transforming compost into flowers. Look at a flower: it is beautiful, it is fragrant, it is pure; but if you look deeply you can already see the compost in the flower. With meditation, you can see that already. If you do not meditate, you will have to wait ten days to be able to see that. If you look deeply at the garbage heap with the eye of a meditator, you can see lettuce, tomatoes, and flowers. That is exactly what the gardener sees when he looks at the garbage heap, and that is why he does not throw away his waste materials. A little bit of practice is all you need to be able to transform the garbage heap into compost and the compost into flowers.

The same is true of our mental formations, which include flowers like faith, hope, understanding, and love; but there is also waste material like fear and pain. The flower is on its way to becoming refuse, but the refuse is also on its way to becoming a flower. This is the nonduality principle of Buddhism: there is nothing to throw away. If a person has never suffered, he or she will never be able to know happiness. If a person does not know what hunger is, he or she will never know the joy of eating every day. Thus pain and suffering are a necessary condition of our understanding, of our happiness. So do not say that you do not want to know anything about pain or about suffering, that you only want to know about happiness—that would be an impossible thing. We know well that suffering helps us to understand, that it nurtures our compassion, and that for this

I must not suppress one side in favor of the other. I know that each of them is vitally necessary for the other. The Buddha tells us: "If this exists, that exists." This exists because that exists. So there should be no conflict, no violence, between one element of our being and another element of our being. There should only be an effort of taking care and being able to transform. So we must have a nonviolent attitude with regard to our suffering, our pain. We must take care of our suffering the way we would take care of our own baby.

We should do that not only in relation to our mental formations but also in relation to our physical body. "Breathing in— I am aware of my eyes. Breathing out—I am smiling at my eyes." When you practice in this way, you touch your eyes with the energy of mindfulness and you begin to make peace with your eyes; you begin to understand the nature of your eyes. If you continue practicing in this way for several minutes, you will see that your eyes are one of the basic conditions for your well-being and your happiness. To have eyes that are still in good condition—what good fortune! This is a marvelous thing. You only have to open your eyes to see the blue sky, the white clouds, the cherry blossoms, the sunset, the face of your baby . . .

With our eyes in good condition, a paradise of forms and colors is available to us. There are people who have lost their sight, and they live in darkness. And they think, they very profoundly believe, that if anybody could help them get their sight back, this would be like entering paradise, the paradise of forms and colors. And we do have our eyes in good functioning order and we really are in a paradise of forms and colors. But without mindfulness, we forget that. Your eyes are already one of the basic conditions of your happiness, and mindfulness helps you to touch one of those conditions.

Let us go on: "Breathing in—I am aware of my heart; breathing out—I am smiling at my heart." "Why, that's very nice," answers your heart. Maybe we have never had the time to do that, and this is the first time we have been aware of our heart. "Dear one, I know that you are there, and I am glad about it." That is the second mantra we learned.

Our heart then begins to experience relief. It has been waiting a very long time for the appearance of this friendly attitude on our part. This evening, we will touch our heart with the energy of mindfulness.

"Breathing in—I know that you are there; breathing out—thank you for being there." If you keep that up for a few minutes, you will perceive that your heart is one of the basic conditions of our happiness. Our heart is still functioning normally—what happiness! Our heart works night and day to preserve our well-being and peace. As for us, we have the time to sleep, but not our heart. Our heart pumps thousands of liters of blood every day so it can irrigate all the cells in our body, without taking a break. Nonetheless, we have not paid enough attention to our heart, and we eat and we drink in such a way that our heart suffers in silence, day and night, year after year. We must turn to our heart and practice the third mantra: "Dear one, I know that you are suffering; that is why I am here for you."

If you continue to practice mindful breathing while deeply touching your heart, you will begin to see things. For example, every time you smoke a cigarette, this is not a friendly gesture toward your heart. Every time you drink alcohol, it is lack of consideration toward your heart. Meditating in this way, you will have wisdom, understanding, and compassion. And if you go on for a week like that, you will stop smoking and drinking.

When somebody comes to us and asks if he or she should stop drinking before receiving the five mindfulness trainings (the precepts), we always tell them that they can continue to drink, but they must drink mindfully. If you drink your wine mindfully for a week, and you practice deeply, you will stop drinking after a few weeks. Nothing is forced on you; it is your own understanding, your wisdom, that tells you how to behave, that tells you how to conduct your everyday life. In Buddhism, when we practice five precepts, or ten, or two hundred and fifty, it's not because the Buddha wants us to do this, but because we are practicing deep looking. We see that practicing the precepts is protecting ourselves against suffering. The precepts are a guarantee of your freedom.

When you touch your liver with mindfulness, you will perhaps begin to hear the SOS put out by your liver. The message sent by your liver is perhaps a very important message. But maybe, because you are not there, the message does not reach you. You have to be there for the person you love. Touching your liver with mindfulness reveals its precise situation, and if you get its message, you will stop drinking and stop eating fats.

The Buddha proposed to us the practice of scanning directed toward the parts of our body. In the sitting position or the lying position, you should use the energy of mindfulness to scan your entire body, starting with your hair and gradually sweeping your body with the energy of mindfulness, the way a scanner does. But the light source here is the light of mindfulness; the energy of mindfulness is the light of the Buddha. You must sweep the entirety of your body, deeply, in order to connect with it and reconcile yourself with it.

I said that we are kings or queens and that our territory is extremely vast. The energy of mindfulness is what makes it possible for us to carry out close surveillance of this territory. We must maintain surveillance of our territory in order to know what is going on there, who is there, what conflicts are there, what wars, what suffering. And it is only through a precise view of your territory that you can manage actually to do something and restore harmony and order there—among the forms, the sensations, the perceptions, the mental formations, and consciousness-knowledge.

the Holy Spirit. Through the Holy Spirit, you come to life again every moment. Mindfulness is the practice that consists in bringing the body and the mind back to the present moment, and every time we practice that, we come to life again.

If we take a look around us, we see people who are living like dead people. Albert Camus says that there are thousands of people moving about around us carrying their own corpses. Thanks to the practice of mindfulness, we come to life again immediately. Being alive is being in the present moment, in the here and now, and that is possible through mindful breathing. In Buddhist meditation, we practice resurrection every moment: "Breathe, you are alive." The Holy Spirit is is present with our mindful breath: "Give us this day our daily bread." This is the very practice of living in the present moment, this day. We must not lose ourselves either in the past or in the future; and the only moment in which we can touch life is the present moment. In Christianity, we find the same teaching as in Buddhism.

When we practice walking meditation, each step brings us back to the present moment. When we walk without mindfulness, we sacrifice the present moment to some destination somewhere—we are not alive. And speaking of destinations, we may as well ask ourselves, what is our final destination? The cemetery, perhaps? In that case, why are we in a hurry to get there? Life does not lie in that direction. Life is here, in each step. For this reason, we must walk in such a way that life arises out of each step, and this is what we do in our community in Plum Village. Not only when we practice formal mindful walking, but throughout the day.

hold yourself back and you run immediately to the phone. In Plum Village, we remain where we are and we consider the sound of the telephone to be like the bell of mindfulness. "Breathing in—I am calming myself; breathing out—I am smiling." Then we go to the telephone in the style of walking meditation, but before that we practice mindful breathing.

In our community, every time we hear a bell, we stop—we stop our thinking, we stop our conversation, we stop our work; and we begin breathing—an inbreath, then an outbreath—and it is the same thing whether it is the telephone ringing or the clock chiming. In this way we have lots of opportunities to return to ourselves, to our true home, here and now, to touch peace. And what we are stopping, in order to be able to be alive, is our thinking. When you contemplate the full moon, if you are thinking then the full moon is not there and you are not there either. This is because thinking prevents us from living deeply in the present moment in our everyday life. When you are drinking water, drink water, drink only water. That is meditation. You must not drink other things, such as your worries, your plans— wandering around in the realm of your thoughts. Thinking prevents us from touching life deeply. I think, therefore I am really not there.

So we remain there when the telephone rings, and we practice. Listen, listen: this wonderful sound brings me back to the present moment. On the third ring, you can go get it, but with dignity and in the style of walking meditation. You breathe, you smile, and you behave in such a way that peace is within you. This is a good thing, not only for you but also for the person who is calling, because you will not be irritated.

If you are the person who is calling, you should do the following—you can learn this little text, or to begin with, put it by your phone, because it can open the door to understanding and bring back harmony: "I am determined to practice deep listening. I am determined to practice loving speech." Each of these two lines corresponds to an inbreath or an outbreath, and after having breathed in this way twice, you will have more calm. You have made a vow to practice attentive listening and to practice loving speech—now you are qualified to dial the number. When the phone rings on the other end, you are not in a hurry, because you know that the other person is in the midst of practicing breathing. Imagine both people practicing smiling and being calm. If everybody in Washington, D.C., would practice that, then the capital would be a much better place to live. Calm, peace, and the smile would be there!

Many of my students who practice telephone meditation have reported back that since they began, not only have things with them personally gone better but their dealings have, too. This is because they have become much nicer. At Plum Village, we established the practice of telephone meditation more than ten years ago, and at the beginning we had certain difficulties. When the phone rang, since everybody loved the practice of mindful breathing, nobody wanted to go answer it. If you telephone Plum Village, you will know that you have a big opportunity to practice mindful breathing.

* * *

To practice hugging meditation, you must practice three mindful breaths, then form a lotus flower with your hands. At the same time the other person also prepares in the same way. And when you take the person you love in your arms, you must practice deeply. "Breathing in—I know that he is alive in my arms; breathing out—I am very glad about it." Three times like that, and you are really there, and the other person is really there too. It is a very pleasant practice, which brings you back to the present moment. Meditating is using the energy of mindfulness so that life will be there as a reality; and amid the agitations of everyday life, Buddhist meditation can be practiced very well.

# Everybody Should Practice Mindfulness

Relief, peace, well-being, joy, and better relations with others will be possible if we practice mindfulness in our everyday life. I am convinced that everybody can practice mindfulness, even politicians, political parties, even the Congress. This is a body that holds the responsibility for knowing the nation's situation well, and knowledge of this kind requires the practice of looking deeply. If our elected officials are not calm enough, do not have enough concentration, how can they see things deeply? If they are not able to listen to the people or to their colleagues in the Congress, if they are not able to speak with loving speech, then there will be much left to be desired. It is necessary for politicians to practice calm, to practice stopping, and to practice looking deeply.

You who are journalists, writers, citizens, you have the right and the duty to say to those you have elected that they must practice mindfulness, calm, deep listening, and loving speech. This is a universal thing, taught by all religions. In Buddhism, we call this *samatha*—stopping, concentration, calm. When calm is there, we are able to practice deep looking.

Let us imagine that the members of the Congress practiced mindful breathing and walking, deep listening, and calm loving speech. As it is, every time they convene, they quarrel and shoot poison arrows, because very few of those people are capable of calming, of practicing loving speech. The situation is very tense; there is a great deal of hatred and anger and discrimination. How is it possible, in such a state, for people to practice deep looking with the aim of achieving a deep knowledge of the nation? So it is necessary to practice mindfulness—it could be Buddhist or Christian—but it is necessary to bring mindfulness to our everyday life. If you are a journalist, a teacher, or a filmmaker, you should practice mindfulness—for the sake of your own calm and your own happiness, but also for that of other people as well. Because we need your calm, your compassion, your understanding. So we should be mindful as individuals but also as a community, as a family, as a nation.

helps us to touch nonfear. It is only here that you can experience total relief, total happiness. Nirvana is the foundation of our being, just as water is considered to be the essence of all waves. In the beginning we think that we have a beginning and an end, a birth and a death, and we might think that before our birth we were not there and after our death we will not be there, and we get caught up in the concept of being and nonbeing. Together let us look deeply at a wave in the ocean. It lives its life of a wave, but it lives the life of water at the same time. If the wave were able to turn toward itself and touch its substance, which is water, then it would be able to attain nonfear and nirvana. We live with the concepts of birth and death, of being and nonbeing, of unity and plurality; we have not had the occasion to touch the ultimate dimension of our being.

This is nirvana, which can be translated as "extinction." But extinction of what? Of all emotions, including the notions of birth, death, being, and nonbeing.

Birth and death cannot touch the bodhisattva, nor the wave once it has realized that at the same time it is water. Concepts such as birth and death, being and nonbeing, might in some sense be applied to waves. As far as water is concerned, these qualifications cannot describe the nature of water. When we speak of birth, of death, of being and nonbeing, we are talking in terms of phenomena. In Buddhism, we call this the historical dimension. When we talk about waves, we are in the historical dimension, but when we talk about water, we are in the ultimate dimension in which we cannot speak of birth and death, of being and nonbeing. The wave might think that before its birth it was not there and that after its death it will not be there, but these are notions—concepts—that cannot be applied in the dimension of the ultimate.

The Buddha declared the following: "There is a world, but there is no birth and there is no death, there is no high and no low, no being and no nonbeing." If that world is not there, how could the world of birth and death, the world of being and nonbeing, be possible? He was talking about the ultimate dimension; he was talking about the water, but all he said was a few words because we cannot use concepts and words with regard to the ultimate.

When we talk about the theology of "God is dead," this means that the notion of God must be dead in order for God to reveal himself as a reality. The theologians, if they only use concepts, words, and not direct experience, are not very helpful. The same goes for nirvana, which is something to be touched and lived and not discussed and described. We have notions that distort truth, reality. A Zen master said the following to a large assembly: "My friends, every time I use the word *Buddha*, I suffer. I am allergic to it. Every time I do it, I have to go to the bathroom and rinse my mouth three times in succession." He said this in order to help his disciples not to get caught up in the notion of Buddha. The Buddha is one thing, but the notion of Buddha is another. Another Zen master said this: "If you meet the Buddha on your way, you must kill him." You have to kill the notion of Buddha so that the real Buddha can be revealed to you. That day, there was a very solid person in the assembly, a monk who stood up and said these words: "Master, every time you say mindfulness, enough practice to touch the foundation of being that is nirvana.

That is why we should do what we have to do to make this meditation of looking deeply a matter of everyday life—when we are eating, when we are drinking, when we are sleeping—and one day we will be able to touch the ultimate reality that is in us. Nirvana is not something that we should search for, because we are nirvana, just as the wave is already water. The wave does not have to search for water, because water is the very substance of the wave. Living deeply makes it possible to touch nirvana, our ultimate reality, the world of no-birth and no-death, and all our fear will be taken away because of this direct knowledge of our true nature.

\* \* \*

I wish for all of you to have a brother or a sister who is a serious practitioner of the Dharma, a spiritual friend who possesses solidity, joy, freedom, understanding, and love. Then your practice will be much more enjoyable, because you will have the support of a sangha, of a practice community, of a being, of brothers and sisters in the Dharma.

# About the Author

THICH NHAT HANH (pronounced "tick not hon") is a world-renowned Zen monk, poet, and peace activist who has been nominated for the Nobel Peace Prize. Born in Vietnam, for the past thirty years he has lived in exile in France, where he founded the monastic community of Plum Village. He has also established Maple Forest Monastery in Vermont and Deer Park Monastery in California. Thich Nhat Hanh travels actively through North America and Europe, teaching "the art of mindful living" to people of all backgrounds. He is the author of numerous books, including the best-selling *The Miracle of Mindfulness, Peace Is Every Step, Anger,* and *Living Buddha, Living Christ.*

*Thich Nhat Hanh's*
*Practice Centers*

*USA*

MAPLE FOREST MONASTERY
(for men and couples)
P.O. Box 354
South Woodstock, VT 05071
Tel.: (802) 457-8170
E-mail: stoneboy@vermontel.net
Website: www.mapleforestmonastery.org

GREEN MOUNTAIN DHARMA CENTER
(for women)
P.O. Box 182
Hartland-Four-Corners, VT 05049
Tel.: (802) 436-1103
E-mail: mfmaster@vermontel.net
Website: www.greenmountaincenter.org

DEER PARK MONASTERY
(for men and couples)
2499 Melru Lane
Escondido, CA 92026
Tel.: (760) 291-1003
E-mail: deerpark@plumvillage.org
Website: www.deerparkmonastery.org


*France*

PLUM VILLAGE, UPPER HAMLET
(for men and couples)
Le Pey, 24240

Thenac, France
Tel.: (33) 5-53-58-48-58
Fax: (33) 5-53-57-49-17
E-mail: UH-office@plumvillage.org
Website: www.plumvillage.org

NEW HAMLET
(for women and couples)
13 Martineau
33580 Dieulivol, France
Tel.: (33) 5-56-61-66-88
Fax: (33) 5-56-61-61-51
E-mail: NH-office@plumvillage.org
Website: www.plumvillage.org

LOWER HAMLET
(for women and couples)
Meyrac 47120
Loubes-Bernac, France
Tel.: (33) 5-53-94-75-40
Fax: (33) 5-53-94-75-90

E-mail: LH-office@plumvillage.org
Website: www.plumvillage.org

SON HA TEMPLE
Fontagnane 24240
Puyguilhem, France
Tel.: (33) 5-53-22-88-89
Fax: (33) 5-53-22-88-90
E-mail: sonha@plumvillage.org
Website: www.plumvillage.org

*Vietnam*

TU HIEU ROOT TEMPLE
Thon Thuong 2
Xa Thuy Xuân—Huyen Huong Thuy
Thua Thiên, Viet Nam
Tel.: (84) 54 826 989
Fax: (84) 54 884 051

LIBRARY OF CONGRESS CATALOGING-IN-PUBLICATION DATA

Nhât Hành, Thích.
[Vivre en Pleine Conscience. English]
True love : a practice for awakening the heart / Thich Nhat Hanh;
translated by Sherab Chödzin Kohn.—1st Shambhala ed.
p. cm.
In English; translated from French.
Originally published: Vivre en Pleine Conscience. Editions Terre
du Ciel, 1997. ISBN 1-59030-188-9 (hardcover: alk. paper)
1. Love—Religious aspects—Buddhism. 2. Compassion—Religious
aspects—Buddhism. 3. Buddhism—Doctrines. I. Chödzin, Sherab.
II. Title.
BQ5359.N53 2004
294.3'5677—dc22
2004006987